LACHLAN PHILPOTT is a Sydney-based writer, dramaturg, teacher and dog person. As a writer he has worked with many theatre and arts companies in Australia, England, France, Kenya, Scotland and the USA. Lachlan has a long-term creative collaboration with director/academic Dr Alyson Campbell who has directed the premieres of several of his new works.

Lachlan's plays include *Bison*, *Bustown*, *Catapult*, *Colder* (winner of the R.E Ross Trust Award), *In 3D*, *Lake Disappointment*, *Michael Swordfish*, *M.ROCK*, *promiscuous/cites*, *Run Rhianna Run!*, *Silent Disco* (winner of the Griffin Award for Outstanding New Australian play, the GAP Competition Aurora Theatre Co. USA, the best stage play, Australian Writers' Guild Awards), *The Chosen*, *Truck Stop* (winner of best play, young audiences Australian Writers' Guild Awards), *The Trouble with Harry* and *Walter*.

Lachlan was awarded an Australia Council Cultural Leadership grant to study new play development models in several countries and was named the inaugural Australian Professional Playwright Fulbright Scholar in 2014/15. Lachlan was Chair of the Australian Writers' Guild Playwrights' Committee between 2012 and 2015.

Daniel Steel as Kieran in Newington College's 2016 production.
(Photo: Christopher Hayles)

MICHAEL SWORDFISH
LACHLAN PHILPOTT

Currency Press, Sydney

CURRENCY PLAYS

First published in 2017
by Currency Press Pty Ltd,
PO Box 2287, Strawberry Hills, NSW, 2012, Australia
enquiries@currency.com.au
www.currency.com.au

Copyright: *A Catalyst for Conversation* © Fraser Corfield, 2017; *Developing Michael Swordfish: Challenging a Narrow View of Masculinity* © Tamara Smith, 2017; *Michael Swordfish* © Lachlan Philpott, 2016, 2017.

COPYING FOR EDUCATIONAL PURPOSES

The Australian *Copyright Act 1968* (Act) allows a maximum of one chapter or 10% of this book, whichever is the greater, to be copied by any educational institution for its educational purposes provided that that educational institution (or the body that administers it) has given a remuneration notice to Copyright Agency Limited (CAL) under the Act.
For details of the CAL licence for educational institutions contact CAL, 11/66 Goulburn Street, Sydney, NSW, 2000; tel: within Australia 1800 066 844 toll free; outside Australia 61 2 9394 7600; fax: 61 2 9394 7601; email: info@copyright.com.au.

COPYING FOR OTHER PURPOSES

Except as permitted under the Act, for example a fair dealing for the purposes of study, research, criticism or review, no part of this book may be reproduced, stored in a retrieval system, or transmitted in any form or by any means without prior written permission. All enquiries should be made to the publisher at the address above.

Any performance or public reading of *Michael Swordfish* is forbidden unless a licence has been received from the author or the author's agent. The purchase of this book in no way gives the purchaser the right to perform the play in public, whether by means of a staged production or a reading. All applications for public performance should be addressed to Elizabeth Troyeur & Associates, 3/66 Oxford St, Darlinghurst NSW 2010, phone: +61 409 658 818, email: elizabeth@troyeur.com.au.

Cataloguing-in-publication data for this title is available from the National Library of Australia website: www.nla.gov.au

Typeset by Dean Nottle for Currency Press.
Cover design by Eugene Designs.
Cover photo by Sam Evans. Photo shows Louis Nicholls.

Currency Press acknowledges the Traditional Owners of the Country on which we live and work. We pay our respects to all Aboriginal and Torres Strait Islander Elders, past and present.

Contents

A Catalyst for Conversation
  Fraser Corfield vii

Developing Michael Swordfish:
Challenging a Narrow View of Masculinity
  Tamara Smith xi

MICHAEL SWORDFISH 1

Fergus Finlayson (left) as Matt and Louis Nicholls as James in Newington College's 2016 production. (Photo: Christopher Hayles)

A Catalyst for Conversation

Australia is experiencing something of a renaissance in theatre for young adults. Since 2010 we have seen plays driven by teenage characters and performed by young actors moving increasingly onto our nation's main stages. There has been a growing awareness that sophisticated stories that reflect the complex world navigated in our teenage years are as compelling as those we experience at any time in our lives.

This has been coupled with the growing recognition that a young actor, though they may lack the technical training and experience that comes with age, brings an authenticity to the portrayal of characters their own age, a truth and vulnerability, that is lost with time. As a result the Australian theatre industry has recognised that we need to see more young people on stage.

An interesting outcome of this change has been a blurring of what was previously considered 'youth theatre'. Where once 'youth theatre' was seen to define the quality of a work or the manner in which it was developed, relegating a production to sit within what was perceived as 'community' or 'amateur' theatre, now we see 'youth theatre' productions in the seasons of our flagship companies.

Lachlan Philpott is one of the Australian playwrights at the heart of this transformation. His work is borne from experience working in professional theatre, of being the Artistic Director of a youth theatre company and from working as a high school teacher. I believe Lachlan Philpott is one of the most significant and original voices in Australian theatre. He fearlessly takes characters not traditionally found on our main stages and demonstrates how compelling and diverse storytelling can be.

Philpott's critically acclaimed plays *Silent Disco*, *Truck Stop* and *MRock* meld a teenage vernacular with a highly poetic narrative form, elevating characters otherwise dismissed as inarticulate or naive to a heightened theatrical eloquence. The everyday struggle for self-esteem, love, belonging and acceptance become epic battles, contrasting grand narratives with very ordinary, recognisable Australians. Philpott shows us that the struggles of our teenage years can be as desperate and significant as any event later in life; often more so. As a result his work has been produced across Australia and is gaining recognition around the world.

In *Michael Swordfish* we see Philpott's trademark complexity and sophistication, this time within a framework that we more readily recognise as 'youth theatre'. Commissioned by Newington College and developed in collaboration with the students of the school, this play is perfectly tailored for a large cast of teenage actors. The script captures the deprecating humour, wit and cruelty of teenage conversations, as well as subtle allusions to more complex relationships and motivations.

Michael Swordfish uses a chorus delivery that switches frequently and effortlessly between direct address to the audience and the interaction between characters. In this way he includes the audience as a character in the play. It is a style of delivery that is perfectly suited to work with young actors. Some of youth theatre's most successful plays apply a similar technique, works such as Noel Greig's *Rainbow's Ending*, Evan Placey's *Girls Like That* and Patricia Cornelius' *Slut*. The rapid-fire delivery of lines maintains energy and a sense of urgency and guards against situations getting bogged down in sentimentality and self-reflection. The intercut narration also allows a larger group of actors to share responsibility for the play, distributing the text more evenly across the performers. It's a very democratic theatrical device.

Of course the danger with this form is that the rapid delivery begins to lack variety in tone and rhythm. There is the danger that the cast, in needing to maintain high performance energy and staying tight on their cues, will feed off one another and lose the individuality and difference in character that is required to give the story light and shade.

But in *Michael Swordfish* we clearly see why Philpott is one of our leading playwrights. While the piece does maintain energy through short lines and direct address, the cast do so within clearly and carefully defined characters. The work is not narrated by a homogenous group of teenage boys. The story is relayed to us by a very specific group of young men who were at the school in question at the time of the events. This clever shift in form allows *Michael Swordfish* to touch on a range of themes with a subtlety and honesty that can't be replicated by a traditional chorus. It allows for glimpses and revelations into the wider world the young men inhabit.

One of the great strengths of *Michael Swordfish* is that it doesn't seek to make an overt political statement or deliver a simplistic moral lesson. Instead it is what all good theatre should be: a catalyst for conversation. The play provokes audiences to reflect on personal notions of responsibility, guilt, inclusion and belonging against the backdrop of broader themes such as death, suicide, sexuality, and family. Once again Philpott draws detailed, ordinary Australians and places them in a grand theatrical context.

Michael Swordfish is an outstanding example of the evolution of youth theatre in Australia. It is a play to challenge young actors and captivate audiences. This work is ideal for secondary schools, universities and youth theatres. This script brings the maturity and complexity we expect in adult professional theatre and offers it to young artists and audiences. I have no doubt it will have many productions over the years to come.

Fraser Corfield
Sydney, 2017

Fraser Corfield is the Artistic Director of the national youth theatre company Australian Theatre for Young People (ATYP).

Fergus Finlayson as Matt, Angus Powell as Sam, Jason Hartill as Toby and Gus Watts as Glen in Newington College's 2016 production. (Photo: Christopher Hayles)

Developing Michael Swordfish: Challenging a Narrow View of Masculinity

Theatre has the power to move and challenge both performer and audience. It can be a mirror, a commentary, or a conversation-starter. It is the perfect antidote to our technologically consumed lives. We are in a unique position in school Drama departments to utilise this powerful tool to engage young minds, encourage conversation and explore the world. Through the process of making and performing theatre, we enter a space where we can explore ideas that can be challenging, dangerous and confronting, but also exciting and fun. With all of these things in mind, Newington College commissioned Lachlan Philpott to work with students on a project that sought to empower the young men of our school through the process of creating and performing an original theatrical work.

In 2014 when this project was in its infancy, there was a lot of talk in the media relating to the coward punch attacks that seemed to be occurring on more than a regular basis here in Sydney. What became quite clear to me was that the public discourse around adolescent males was, and unfortunately still is, largely pessimistic. This bothered me because my experience here with the young men at Newington was and still is the total opposite. These boys are willing to buck the trend and challenge the stereotypes associated with being a man. They are articulate and willing in their discussions about their worlds and their ideas. The lack of youth and student perspective sought and publicised regarding these issues that directly relate to them both surprises and saddens me. In her *Sydney Morning Herald* article, *No Country for Young Men: Notions of Gender Must Evolve* (January 3, 2014), Professor Catharine Lumby called for a challenge to society's 'narrow idea of masculinity'. At Newington, that is what we set out to do.

The process of creating this piece, in collaboration with Lachlan, gave the voices of the young men involved (an organic mixture of experienced Drama students and those new to Drama) a forum in which they were heard, recognised and valued. The process of guiding the students through potentially turbulent and difficult subject matter was both a privilege and an eye-opener. Away from the constraints of assessment schedules, marks and outcomes, we were able to drill down into the things that mattered most to the boys and began exploring ways to communicate these on stage.

We have had over fifty students contribute to this project in its two-year development. The process included a number of discussion groups and surveys, talking about issues, characters and points of view. We felt it was important that we didn't rush to get boys on their feet. Instead, we took the time to listen to their ideas and the things that resonate with them. As a result, the boys felt proud that their voices were being heard and took the responsibility very seriously, wanting to ensure that what was ultimately presented on stage was a true representation of their lives, opinions and passions.

The first few months of the process was spent asking questions like:

- What are some of the stereotypes associated with young men?
- What are some of the realities about being a young man today?
- What does it mean to be masculine?
- What do you wish adults knew about teenagers today?

We also asked the boys to explore a number of discussion starters:

- It bothers me that …
- Boys should avoid crying in front of people.
- Boys shouldn't ask for help.
- It's okay to use intimidation to get the job done.
- It's the boy's job to ask a girl out.
- It's important to act cool and calm even when feeling afraid.
- Drinking to excess is cool.
- It's okay to discriminate against someone based on their sexuality.
- If I need to talk about my feelings or emotions, I talk to Mum over Dad.
- You should get back at people who disrespect you.
- A man should avoid crying in front of people.
- Creative pursuits aren't very manly.
- Muscles and physical strength are the measure of a man.
- Being reckless is just part of being a boy.
- I'm comfortable with not fitting in with the male stereotype.
- It is important to stand up when things are wrong.

The responses were surprising, inspiring, mature, confronting, and honest. They provided a number of different characters, situations and relationships that Lachlan could then begin exploring in his writing. Responses as insightful as:

I wish adults knew that ...
- If we want space, we need it.
- We have our own ideas for the future.
- We make mistakes just like everyone else.
- Your experiences as a teenager don't always relate to our experiences as a teenager.
- Give us time, we'll grow up.
- We like to be taken seriously.
- Your experiences don't dictate what I want.
- Just leave me alone!
- I don't need to be understood.
- We can make our own choices.

The authentic voices that Lachlan has captured in the pages of this play are a result of the many hours of listening and working with the boys to understand what really makes them tick. In treating the boys as artists, equals in the creative process and genuinely respecting every idea and offer they made, no matter how ridiculous or brilliant, he has been able to capture the voices of the boys involved perfectly; their ridiculous language and hilarious banter through to their profound and sensitive ideas. There is life in the nine characters of the play far beyond the pages of the script.

This is a play that we are incredibly proud of. Throughout the entire process, the boys were so completely engaged with the piece because it is a true and realistic representation of the issues they experience or see their mates grapple with on a day-to-day basis. For the adults in the audience—parents, teachers, and family members—it at times felt confronting. However, it was a chance for them to listen, hearing it directly from the boys.

This project is grounded in their world and we should be proud and inspired by their constantly evolving, insightfully mature and powerful ideas about who they are and the world that they are inheriting. Our hope is that through this work, we can give voice to those 'characters' that have trouble finding acceptance and tolerance; those who not only have something to say but need a chance to say it. And to be heard.

When we set out to create this play, it was never our intention for it to focus on one central character. Despite what the title of the play might suggest, *Michael Swordfish* is about so much more than just Michael. James, Glen, Matt, Toby, Sam, Kieran, Tristan, Henry and Michael together represent the voices of a multitude of teenage boys. This project was a remarkable experience and journey for all involved and the Newington College community will be eternally grateful to Lachlan for his willingness to help tell the stories of our boys and give voice to their fears and dreams.

Tamara Smith
Sydney, 2017

Tamara Smith is Head of Drama at Newington College.

Michael Swordfish was commissioned by Newington College and first produced at Newington College Drama Theatre, Sydney, on 18 July 2016, with the following cast:

TRISTAN	Eden Bradford
HENRY	Ashutosh Bidkar
MATT	Fergus Finlayson
TOBY	Jason Hartill
MICHAEL	Tim Kenzler
JAMES	Louis Nicholls
SAM	Angus Powell
KIERAN	Daniel Steel
GLEN	Gus Watts

Director, Tamara Smith
Set and Costume Designer, Tamara Smith
Lighting Designer, Richard Neville
Sound Designers, Nick Fitzsimmons and Ben Taylor
Production Assistant, Ben Williams

CHARACTERS

    JAMES
    GLEN
    TOBY
    MATT
    SAM
    KIERAN
    TRISTAN
    HENRY
    MICHAEL

Nine male actors, aged about 17, play these roles.

HENRY is Singaporean and could be of Chinese or Indian background.

The others can be who they are. I encourage casting actors who can reflect the diversity of our evolving culture.

Some of the actors will need to take on the voices of other characters. These characters are STONE, DEZZY, PERCIVAL, MISS, JULIA, SHANNON, CASSIE, GIRL, and CATHY. For the most part they needn't 'become' the actual character in anything much more than a shift of vocal quality and the use of gestures and presence. But it might be fun to play about and find what works for you.

SETTING

On stage there could be a large structure that can be climbed. Perhaps it's made of twisted school chairs and desks or things from childhood. This structure could be destroyed by GLEN and SAM when they have a rampage towards the end of the play.

TEXT NOTE

/ denotes a point of interruption and generally indicates overlapping dialogue. Dialogue after the first / begins at the same time as dialogue after the second.

Dialogue in italics is reported speech: a line that the boys are quoting from someone else.

All characters are fictional and any resemblance to actual people is unintentional.

Back Row: Gus Watts as Glen, Fergus Finlayson as Matt, Ashutosh Bidkar as Henry, Daniel Steel as Kieran.
Front Row: Louis Nicholls as James, Eden Bradford as Tristan, Jason Hartill as Toby, Angus Powell as Sam.
Newington College's 2016 production. (Photo: Christopher Hayles)

MICHAEL *stands before us. Then there is a moment, perhaps a flash of light at which point he vanishes, to be replaced by the eight others:* JAMES, GLEN, TOBY, MATT, SAM, KIERAN, TRISTAN, *and* HENRY.

JAMES: It's Wednesday morning and the last week of term.
SAM: We're in the middle of PE.
TRISTAN: About to win footy when Prior gets this note.
JAMES: He reads it.
TRISTAN: Blows his whistle.
SAM: *Assembly. Change back into your uniforms.*
TRISTAN: What?
JAMES: Now, sir?
TRISTAN: But we're about to / win.
TOBY: / What's happened, sir?
SAM: He shakes his head.
JAMES: Something's happened you can tell.
SAM: Shakes his head again.
JAMES: Because they don't just call assembly like that.
SAM: Takes the ball back. Says: / *Move. Don't make a fuss.*
TRISTAN: / *Move. Don't make a fuss.*
GLEN: Note held above Mrs Petrie's head. Face red, she tells us:
KIERAN: / *Close the books.*
HENRY: / *Close the books, put Iago away, pack him up and go to the hall.*
JAMES: And a normal day.
TRISTAN: A Wednesday just like the rest changes into something else. / Something's happened.
MATT: / Something's happened.
TOBY: On the way to the hall I see clouds in the sky make a question mark above. It asks why.
MATT: Hurry up, Toby.

> TOBY *follows* MATT.
>
> *The eight boys are at assembly.*

GLEN: In the hall.
HENRY: We scuff and fiddle and muck about.
JAMES: Harley's on stage under the flags.

GLEN: Look at his face.
TRISTAN: Do I have to?
KIERAN: Face screwed up like a pit bull.
MATT: He looks worried.
KIERAN / SAM: He's not glaring like he usually does.
TOBY: What's wrong with him?
GLEN: Maybe there's a war.
TRISTAN: Good one, Glen.
GLEN: Like ISIS.
TRISTAN: And they're sending you to Syria!
GLEN: They've declared war and we all have to go and fight.
TRISTAN: Right, Glen!
JAMES: These Year Eight boys have heard Glen and they stare at him.
TRISTAN: Scaring the little 'uns. mate.
GLEN: Or maybe some kid's gone wild, gone jihad or insurgent or —
TOBY / MATT: Shut up, Glen.
TRISTAN: Hey, it's Glen's farewell assembly. He's off to special needs school.
KIERAN: Ha!
JAMES: Miss Jones from the office crosses the stage.
GLEN: Look at the Doberman.
HENRY: We call Jones that.
GLEN: Nazi guard dog who runs the school.
TRISTAN: The Doberman whispers something to Harley.
GLEN: Wonder what she's saying?
SAM: *Come and meet me in the book room.*
GLEN: Yuck!
TRISTAN: Then she leaves him alone on the stage.
TOBY: The whole school falls silent.
MATT: And then Freddy comes in late. He's on crutches again and / everyone laughs.
TOBY: / Everyone laughs, but then sound's shot dead.
JAMES: 'Cause / Jones leads in two cops.
KIERAN: / Jones leads in two cops.
GLEN: Cops. Cops. Cops.
TRISTAN: Yeah, Glen. / Cops.
GLEN: / Cops.

TOBY: One woman.
JAMES: One man.
GLEN: She's hot. Is she hot?
SAM: Cops look solemn, not mean.
HENRY: And the hall is on mute, everyone's muted / sound right down.
MATT: / Everyone's still.
JAMES: You can't even hear Zimmerman wheeze.
SAM: Teachers hover at the edges, don't know what's going down.
JAMES: And it's quiet like forever.
TOBY: A whole blue sky full of quiet, no question mark now just a big wide space.
MATT: Harley clears his throat.
TRISTAN: He doesn't start with the usual jokes, just looks out at us and says:
SAM: *Good morning, boys. I'm sorry to say that / I have some disturbing news.*
KIERAN: / *I have some disturbing news. / About a boy.*
SAM: / *About a boy.*
JAMES / TRISTAN: About a boy from this school.
SAM / KIERAN: *This morning, as you can see we have the police here and ...*
MATT: What's happened?
GLEN: A murder.
TRISTAN: Glen!
GLEN: Well, what else? It's death, I know, someone's died, someone's—
KIERAN: I'm wondering how bad it'll be—
TRISTAN: What year? Who is this going to hit?
HENRY: A plane roars right over the hall.
TOBY: Mr Harley searches for words to say in the empty space above our heads.
MATT: Who hasn't been in class?
GLEN: See? Someone's dead?
SAM: Was there an accident?
JAMES: No-one said.
KIERAN: Did someone die?
TRISTAN: Look up and down the rows to see if there is a sign, an empty space.

SAM: Wonder who?
JAMES: Which year, which class which—
MATT: 'Cause last year a kid died and the school fell apart, is that what's going on again?
TOBY: Then Harley says:
HENRY: *This morning the school was informed that a student has not been seen for a long enough time to be reported as missing.*

    Beat.

GLEN: No-one's dead.
JAMES: And the stuff he says next blurs because / all we want to know is who.
MATT: / All we want to know is who. / The name.
JAMES: / The name.
TRISTAN: The year.
MATT / JAMES: All we want to know is the name.

    Beat.

TOBY / TRISTAN: Michael Swordfish.
JAMES: Harley finally says.
MATT / TOBY: Michael Swordfish.
KIERAN: *I have to let you all know that this morning we received the troubling news that / Michael Swordfish—*
JAMES: / Michael Swordfish has not been seen since Sunday afternoon and the police have come to speak to you because we will need all the help we can get to find Michael. And we will. / We will find Michael Swordfish.
HENRY: / We will find Michael Swordfish.

    A beat.

    A shift in light and mood.

TRISTAN: There are kids you notice because of the way they look.
SAM: Handsome guys who everyone sees.
MATT: Kids you can't ignore because of the way they behave.
JAMES: Kids whose names are plastered on boards in halls.
GLEN: Or toilet walls.
TOBY: And then there are other kids.
JAMES: Kids like Michael.
SAM: I know he's in our year.

MATT: He's tall with a quiet voice.
TOBY: Blond hair. Green eyes.
GLEN: He's in my Physics class.
KIERAN: He does French.
SAM: Is he in Art?
TOBY: He sometimes takes our train.
HENRY: Dark hair. Maybe Lebanese.
TOBY: You see him down the end of the platform.
MATT: Short hair.
KIERAN: Brown eyes.
TOBY: He keeps to himself.
GLEN: He gets to school late.
TRISTAN: You see teachers catching him late at the gate.
MATT: He's in our French class.
TOBY: Madame Dufoyet called him / Monsieur Poisson-Epée.
MATT: / *Monsieur Poisson-Epée.* She thought she was funny but no-one understood.
GLEN: The police lady looks at our row, she looks at me as she speaks into the mic.
JAMES: She tells us her name is Constable Kelly Clarkson.

    Some of the boys laugh.

GLEN: What?
TOBY: Kelly Clarkson stares out at us and blinks.
GLEN: What's so funny? Who's …?
TOBY: Kelly Clarkson says that the last time Michael was seen was on Sunday.
MATT: He was at the end of the street where he lives.
JAMES: Not far from here.
SAM: He was sitting on the gutter in the corner just / staring at his phone.
MATT: / Staring at his phone.
TOBY: And then he wasn't there anymore. There was just a space where he was sitting.
KIERAN: No-one's found the phone. They've been ringing it but now the battery's dead.
HENRY: Kelly Clarkson says when someone goes missing it's best to act fast.

JAMES: *Think about Michael.* She says.
MATT: Think about anything you know which might help.
TOBY: She tells us she'll be here all day at the school and if anyone knows anything, anything at all,
TRISTAN: If we saw something here,
GLEN: Or online,
TOBY: On Facebook or Snapchat,
KIERAN: Twitter or …
TRISTAN: So impressive, she knows them all.
SAM: That if we saw something, know something …
JAMES: Any detail. Anything at all, we should say.
KIERAN: Harley takes the mic back and tells us that there's / a box.
SAM: / A box outside the office.
KIERAN: A box with Michael's name on it.
SAM: So we can write something anonymously about Michael if we need.
GLEN: Like what?
KIERAN: Information, Glen.
GLEN: Right, so why not just say it?
KIERAN: If we know something that you think they need to know.
SAM: But don't want to say.
HENRY: Or don't know how to say because sometimes / it's hard to say things.
TOBY: / It's hard to say things.
MATT: Write it and put it in the Michael box.
KIERAN: The coward's box.
TRISTAN: Yeah, the box for the gutless.

> *Beat.*
>
> *We see a fragment of* MICHAEL*'s face for a moment. Something almost subliminal.*
>
> SAM *places something in the coward's box while* MICHAEL *watches on.*
>
> *The bell rings.*

TOBY: At recess we sit on those seats near the chapel.
MATT: Kelly Clarkson's alone at a table outside the hall.
TOBY: Doberman brings her a cup of tea.

They look in their lunch boxes.

MATT: You want some of this?
TOBY: What is it?
MATT: Dunno. My sister made it.
TOBY: Your sister still got that skin thing?
MATT: Yeah.
TOBY: No thanks.

    MATT *casts it aside.*

How can a kid just go missing?
MATT: Happens. You see it on the news.
TOBY: No.
MATT: Happens in Queensland all the time.
TOBY: Why?

    MATT *shrugs.*

MATT: Queensland.
TOBY: But they find them? I mean the kids come back?
MATT: Don't know. People get bored waiting to find out so it doesn't make the news …
TOBY: Wow. So, who does Michael hang with?
MATT: Don't know. Never see him out of class. When did you last see him out of class?
TOBY: Dunno.
MATT: See. They said he was here last week so maybe then?
TOBY: But did you see him?
MATT: Maybe out of the corner of my eye. Not like there are tapes you can review.
TOBY: No. But … I have this feeling that he's been taken.
MATT: Here we go …
TOBY: That he was sitting in the gutter and a black car pulled up.
MATT: Like …
TOBY: CIA or Men in Black or I dunno.
MATT: Good one, Toby. You always come up with the weirdest shit. He's probably hiding under his bed or …
TOBY: What?

    MATT *doesn't know.*

HENRY: By the afternoon rumours fly around about Michael.

KIERAN: He was caught up in drugs—
TRISTAN: His parents had him on suicide watch.
SAM: He's left the country.
GLEN: His sister was taken too and they sent her bits in a box to the mum and dad.
SAM: Glen!
GLEN: What? It's what I heard.
JAMES: Teachers give nothing away.
HENRY: Gannon's face like a gravestone.
TRISTAN: Know anything, sir? When did they tell you?
JAMES: Gannon doesn't want to talk about it, just writes:
TRISTAN: *Explain how Nazi foreign policy contributed to the upsurge of nationalism between 1934 and 1941.*
JAMES: And says: / *Get on with it.*
TRISTAN: / *Get on with it.*
KIERAN: But it's the biggest thing that's happened in school since …
TRISTAN: And all Gannon wants to talk about is the boring Third Reich.
HENRY: That's so last century.
KIERAN: Remember what happened last year?
MATT: Mitchell Strong.
TOBY: Yeah.
 The assembly when they told us he'd got hit by a taxi driver who had fallen asleep at the wheel.
MATT: And the school just stopped. Kids went pale and quiet and stood in hallways and the teachers stopped teaching.
GLEN: I saw Mr Peachy crying that day. He was sobbing near the gym doors.
MATT: So?
GLEN: Just …
MATT: Everyone was sad, Glen.
TOBY: Yeah. Of course Mitchell was like the fastest back in the firsts.
MATT: That's not why.
GLEN: No.
MATT: It was different.
TOBY: Was it?
MATT: Yes. He died, Toby.
GLEN: Yeah.

MATT: Mitchell died. It was a horrible accident.
TOBY: And he was a prefect and he played with the firsts.
MATT: It doesn't matter what he did.
TOBY: Doesn't it?
MATT: No.
TOBY: Then why are we going on with class today?
MATT: Because Michael's not …
TOBY: What?
MATT: Dead. It's not like Michael's dead. Fuck.
TOBY: What?

> MATT *shakes his head. The bell rings.*

KIERAN: Between History and Maths at the lockers.
SAM: What are they doing?
KIERAN: Sergeant and some of the maintenance guys there with bolt-cutters.
GLEN: What's going on?
SAM: They're cutting the padlock. Is that his locker?
KIERAN: Must be.
GLEN: They must be looking for clues.
SAM: In his locker? Here?
KIERAN: Like what'll they find?
GLEN: Brick of heroin.
SAM: Or a mandarin he didn't eat? Like what clues get left in a locker here?
GLEN: I don't know. Look at the stuff they're pulling out.
KIERAN: Just sweaty old socks and shit.
SAM: They better not start searching all the lockers.
GLEN: Why would they?
KIERAN: What you got hidden?
SAM: Nothing.

> SAM *and* GLEN *look at each other.* KIERAN *goes.*

GLEN: Where are those DVDs I lent you?
SAM: It's okay, mate.
GLEN: You took them home?
SAM: Yeah, but …
GLEN: You brought them back?

SAM: Yeah. Burnt them. I was going to return them to you.
Want them?
GLEN: Not now! They're my brother's if they get confiscated ... Man! I told you not to— [bring them back here]
SAM: Chill. They won't search.
GLEN: They're in your locker. Your risk, not mine. But if they find them—
SAM: Shit, they didn't even work.
GLEN: What?
SAM: All scratched.
GLEN: They were not.
SAM: Chill.
GLEN: No. How can you be so ...? If they find them I know nothing, / man ...
SAM: / Chill, Glen. Just ... they aren't going to search our lockers.
GLEN: Nah.

Beat.

SAM: Kim went missing, you know.
GLEN: Your sister?
SAM: Yeah.
GLEN: When?
SAM: Ages ago. Like when she was like eight.
Mum left the front door open and she ran away like a dog. I still remember the way Mum screamed her name when nobody could find her. *Kim! Kim!*
In the end they had police choppers and the whole neighbourhood scouring the bush.
GLEN: But they found her?
SAM: At Westfield.
GLEN: Random.
SAM: Yeah.
GLEN: Which one?
SAM: Westfield Parramatta. In the food court. We still don't know how she got out there.
GLEN: Westfield Parramatta?
SAM: In front of Donut King eating chicken nuggets. I reckon she'd been kidnapped and whoever took her realised what an annoying bitch she is and changed their minds and dumped her.

GLEN: Too far!
SAM: Nah, you don't have to live with her, man, she's a liability.
GLEN: Your mum and dad must have been worried.

    SAM *shrugs*.

So did she have money on her?
SAM: What?
GLEN: Just … how do you reckon she bought nuggets?
SAM: Kim always gets what she wants.
GLEN: Your parents went to the police?
SAM: Of course they did. She was eight. No-one had seen her for hours and …
GLEN: How does a kid just …?
SAM: When Kim was little she had one of those leads 'cause she always vanished. Dad called her Houdini.
GLEN: What's that mean?
SAM: I don't know. After that happened … she wouldn't say, she wouldn't tell anyone where she'd been or … nothing, no matter what they asked so … they've been tying her since.
GLEN: Bullshit.
SAM: Nah, they have to.
GLEN: How?
SAM: They tie her up at night.
GLEN: Like to her bed?
SAM: No, to the oven, Glen. Of course to her bed.
GLEN: What for?
SAM: To keep her safe.
GLEN: Wow.
SAM: They have to, man.
GLEN: On her back?
SAM: No, on her side.
GLEN: Serious?
SAM: Better than the front.
GLEN: She'd suffocate.
SAM: Yeah.
GLEN: No joke?
SAM: Why would I make that up?

GLEN: Just seems …
SAM: What?
GLEN: Hard core.
SAM: Yeah. Hadn't thought of it like that.
GLEN: Can't they medicate her or something?
SAM: They don't want the side effects. Who wants unwanted side effects? And you get used to shit, you know.
GLEN: So Kim's used to it?
SAM: Yeah. It's a ritual. A story and then they tie her down. You should see her face.
GLEN: Have you seen the exorcist?
SAM: Not like that.
GLEN: How old is she now?
SAM: Eleven.
GLEN: Is that legal?
SAM: Cops suggested it. Keeps her safe.
GLEN: Right.
SAM: Maybe don't tell the others about this.
GLEN: Nah. Okay. Glad I'm not a chick.
SAM: Yeah. Reckon Kim'll be into S&M when she gets older.

GLEN doesn't know how to react to that one.

He watches the policewoman.

GLEN: What you think of her?
SAM: The cop? Poor thing with a name like that, hey?
GLEN: Yeah …
SAM: You don't know what I'm talking about, do you, Glen?
GLEN: Yeah. Kelly Clarkson's like a …
SAM: What?

GLEN doesn't have a clue.

She's like a porn star, Glen.
GLEN: No? Her?

SAM shakes his head.

SAM: Go to class, mate.

SAM goes.

GLEN: But I can't go to Geography 'cause Kelly Clarkson's looking my way. And either the sun is in her eyes or she's smiling like right at me …

A dreamy moment with music.

And snap and he's back.

He goes.

HENRY: So I'm in Art, right. I like that best.
We're doing our major works. Miss Stone wanders around like she does. Kind of sideways. Like a crab. Whispering things to improve our terrible paintings.

MATT: She's not meant to tell us stuff like that / but …

HENRY: / But Stone doesn't care. You can tell she's really an artist not a teacher. Stone's kind of nervy, like fiddly with her hands. She's like a praying mantis. The way she …

They watch her.

MATT: Look at her face. Miss Stone is a stoner.

JAMES: Don't say that about her, Matt, it's so obvious and dumb.

HENRY: Miss Stone keeps looking up to the back of the room.

JAMES: There's this canvas there.

MATT: A canvas on an easel covered in a cloth.

HENRY: Was that there last week?

JAMES: Dunno.

MATT: Wasn't covered if it was.

JAMES: No. What is that, Miss? Under the cover? Miss?

She doesn't respond.

MATT: She's nicked an Arthur Boyd from that place we went—

JAMES: Good one, Matt.

MATT: You know how she was …

JAMES: I want to know what it is …

MATT: Now?

JAMES: Lift up the cover.

MATT: You go.

JAMES: Me? No.

They look at HENRY.

MATT / JAMES: Henry!
JAMES: Go! Now!
    She isn't looking. She isn't. She isn't. / She isn't, she isn't, she isn't …
MATT: / Take off the cover, you dick.

    HENRY *is caught by* STONE.

JAMES: She is …
STONE: *Why did you boys do that?*
HENRY: Sorry, Miss. I don't know.
MATT: We dared him to, Miss. Sorry …
STONE: *It was covered for a reason.*
JAMES: Why, Miss?
STONE: *That doesn't matter right now.*
HENRY: Thanks, guys.

    They stare at the painting.

MATT: It's just a landscape.
JAMES: It's good. The trees and there's a path,
HENRY: The path seems easy to climb at first but …
MATT: It gets smaller as it goes.
JAMES: Bumpier and the sky gets …
MATT: Darker. The light really changes.
JAMES: It looks kind of desolate.
MATT: [*mimicking*] *It looks kind of desolate.*
JAMES: Shut up!
HENRY: Who did it, Miss? Did you?
STONE: *Back to work!*
HENRY: And I see it. I don't say it.
MATT: But who painted this, Miss?
HENRY: 'Cause most of the boys have already turned away. And that's when it hits me.
JAMES: Is it Michael's?
HENRY: When I realise why Miss has covered it up.
JAMES: That's when I see the figure in it. Lost?
HENRY: The figure staring out.
JAMES: Hidden? Lost?
HENRY: The figure in his painting staring out as if to say, 'What?'

JAMES: It's Michael's, isn't it, Miss?
MATT: Wow. I never knew Swordfish could paint.
JAMES: When did he do this?
HENRY: Why was it covered up, Miss?
MATT: Never saw him painting in class.
HENRY: Yeah, he comes in and paints at lunch.
MATT: Who with?

>*They both look at* JAMES. MICHAEL *appears.*

>GLEN *places something in the coward's box while* MICHAEL *watches on.*

>*The bell rings.* MICHAEL *disappears.*

TOBY: The day ends.
TRISTAN: Kids pile out the school.
KIERAN: Teachers yelling to tuck shit in and: / *Watch the road.*
MATT: / *Watch the road!*
KIERAN: Mothers wait in cars.
MATT: Traffic crawls through the school zone.
HENRY: Kids get into cars and tell their mums about Michael.
TOBY: Grey clouds gather. I stand at the station and see the rain in the distance.
MATT: Train pulling in and / a storm on the way.
TOBY: / A storm on the way. Push into the train.

>*A clap of thunder.*

KIERAN: Rush into the train.
TOBY: It's packed.
KIERAN: Heaps of girls. Hey, Tobes, look who it is up the end.
MATT: Ooooh! Can't miss that red hair, can you, boys?
KIERAN: Go and speak to her.
TOBY: No.
MATT: Annie!
KIERAN: Annie!
TOBY: Fuck off! Shut up.
MATT: Annie! She's looking for you, mate.
KIERAN: *The sun'll come out tomorrow.*
MATT: Wave to her.
KIERAN: *Bet your bottom dollar that tomorrow …*

MATT: Wave. Annie? Annie!
TOBY: STOP IT, GUYS! LEAVE HER ALONE!

We hear a train move through a storm.

HENRY: Rain drums on the roof of the boarding house. Cars splash through puddles on the road.
And I'm thinking if Michael's out there …
If Michael is out there, then … where can he be? If he was taken at least he's dry, but what if he ran away? Is he still on the move? Maybe he hitchhiked? Maybe he's sitting in some truck driving through the fading light. Is he conscious? Does he even know it's raining? Has he got somewhere to sleep tonight? Does he know where he is? Does he want to be there or is he stunned in some pool of his own sick somewhere, the world a blur around him?

All the boys are in their own moment.

TOBY / SAM: I tell Mum.
MATT / GLEN: I tell Dad.
TRISTAN: I don't say a word about it.
SAM: She's making dinner.
GLEN: He's driving home.
SAM: Beef fajitas. Kim's picking at the meat. She'll tie you up early, you hog!
MATT: Dad's lying on the couch watching the news.
SAM: Sour cream blobs into a bowl as Mum yells at Kim. See!
TOBY: Mum's on the phone and she says: *Help! I can't do ten things at once.*
JAMES: Mum's the only one home.
TOBY: I count the things she's doing. One, two, three.
MATT: I tell him about Michael.
TOBY: Three not ten. / Mum looks at me and says: *Missing?*
JAMES: / Mum looks at me and says: / *Missing?*
SAM / GLEN: / *Missing?*
SAM: Mum pushes Kim outside: *Go and watch TV. What's going on, Sam?*
MATT: Nothing on the news about him.
GLEN: *He'll show up, mate. This sort of thing must happen all the time.*
JAMES: Mum asks: *Was there a note or something?* / From him?
TOBY: / *From him?*

JAMES: It's not like that, Mum.
TOBY: *From the school?*
JAMES: *Tell me what they said in assembly.*
SAM: *A police officer in the school?*
GLEN: Like '21 Jump Street'. Except she's a lady. She's nice. She's really kind and funny and you'll never guess what her name is. Nah. Doesn't matter.
HENRY: Mum calls. Three hours behind there, but it sometimes feels further. I don't mention Michael Swordfish 'cause it's bedtime here and she's just leaving work. I wonder what she's making for dinner. Imagine my sister out shopping, watching the clock to beat Mum home, pretend she was studying. / I google 'Michael Swordfish'.
KIERAN / TRISTAN: / I google 'Michael Swordfish'.
KIERAN: Just lots of photos of plates of fish.
TRISTAN: He has no Facebook.
KIERAN: Chefs holding big long platters of fish.
TRISTAN: What kind of a kid has no Facebook?
HENRY: There's no record of him online.
TRISTAN: There's a Linda Swordfish on Facebook.
JAMES: I don't want to talk to Mum about this.
TRISTAN: Linda lives in Mauritius. I send a friend request.
JAMES: I'm thinking of the painting in the Art room.
TRISTAN: Linda's online. Come on, Linda.
JAMES: That place Michael painted.
TRISTAN: Come on, Linda, be my friend.
    Guess she's busy. / I google 'missing teenage boy Sydney'.
HENRY: / I google 'missing teenage boy Sydney'.
JAMES: The path, the road, the changing light.
TRISTAN: No sign of Michael but / there are pages and pages of kids who've gone missing.
HENRY: / There are pages and pages of kids who've gone missing. / Rain pounds down on the roof.
TOBY: / Rain pounds down on the roof.
JAMES: Mum gets a call and I go to my room.
KIERAN: Dad comes home late.
JAMES: Watch Charlie's window. He's not home tonight.
KIERAN: Dad asks: *Did you eat?*

JAMES: Just the glow of something charging on his bed.
KIERAN: I point at the pizza box and Dad rolls his eyes.
JAMES: The rain running down his windows, my windows.
TOBY: Hope Michael's got shelter.
KIERAN: Dad goes straight to his office. Something due.
JAMES: Wish I could go over and knock on Charlie's door.
KIERAN: Dad's closes his office door.
JAMES: Go and sit on his bed.
KIERAN: I close mine too.
JAMES: Sit on his bed and ask him what he thinks about Michael. All the things I want to say.
KIERAN: I stare at the screen at Black Ops III and I shoot and I shoot and I shoot. In zombie mode MR6 is running hot—shoot!
    dead
    dead
    dead
    dead
    zombie juice spatters and sprays
    dead dead dead dead dead dead dead dead dead dead dead dead.
    Dead.
    Dead.
    Dead!

An interlude.

They all leave except for GLEN.

GLEN: What's going on for me right now? Not much. Just you know, getting through school and shit. Shit, can I say that—shit I mean?
Cool.
School's okay. I don't love it or anything. Like if I got off the train and walked up the street and it had vanished one morning I wouldn't cry or anything. Yeah. Some guys would because it's their whole lives and everything. It can be like that, right.
The best things? The sport I guess. I do rowing. And cadets. I like cadets. I don't want to be in the army or anything like that. It's just about getting away. I like that you can get away in the bush and you don't get watched all the time, you get trusted not supervised and you have to survive and the discipline of surviving is what gets you

through. I'm a CUO. My brother was one too. That's not the reason I wanted to be one. I don't have to do everything Seb does.

But it's like at school you get a certain amount of respect if you make it through and who doesn't want that? Respect.

Seb's two years older than me. He finished school last year, he's away on a gap year. Everyone always asks me where he is and I say Russia. I don't know if he's actually even going to Russia. Can you still go there? Mum writes posts to him and says hi or whatever for me. I don't have time to write right now.

I like that Seb's not at school now. It's not like we don't get on. It's just that Seb took up a lot of space 'cause he's really good at everything and I will never be as tall or as smart or as strong and ...

I was a twin when I was born. Maybe that's why. Some people say I will always be a twin but my twin Lachlan was stillborn so he never got to see the world at all. There should have been four brothers. Seb, me, dead Lachlan and Ned. I never got to know if he would have been a Lach or Lachy or Lacho or ...

If Lachlan had have lived we would have been a power block. Like: *Keep your hands off my twin or you die!*

I wonder what would have happened if Lachlan had have lived instead of me. Is that what makes me weak? Half of my life force got cut short and the joy of me arriving in the world was cut just after my cord. They'd bought a double pram and it's still in the back of the garage covered in dust and huntsmen's webs.

Mum always wanted a daughter. You can see it in her face sometimes. If any of us had been a girl they were going to call us Gay. We all dodged a bullet there.

> SAM *enters and plays guitar. He's trying to pick a tune. He always seems to act like people are watching.*

There have been times when I thought Lachlan might just walk up the driveway and knock on the front door and say it was all a big prank and he's back now. That he'll be lying under the bed in my room waiting to jump out and scare the shit out of me. But instead there is just this space.

There are two living twins in the year below us.

The Leopard twins. Jack and Nick. They have spots. On their faces. They do everything together.

I wonder if Lachlan would have been like that with me.

Mum makes a fuss of my birthday to help cover up the sadness. And now Seb's gone. Which I know is totally different because he was like everywhere in my life—at school and at home—and Lachlan … When we saw Seb off at the airport he had a strange look on his face as he went through Customs and I said what would it be like if we never saw him again. Mum didn't find it very funny.

Mum's been standing in the door of Seb's room staring at his bed and Dad keeps saying: *Stop being morbid*. Went through Seb's things. I found some porn. All these DVDs and retro shit.

I have his big TV and shit all set up in my room now.

A shift, indicating a new day.

JAMES: It rains all night.
TOBY: Thursday. Train full of umbrellas.
GLEN: Dad drives me to school.
TRISTAN: Mum drives me to school. At the red lights I watch this woman and her dog in a rusty car next to us. She's smoking with the windows up, poisoning her dog. Mum and me never know what to say to each other.
JAMES: I get off at the station and …
TRISTAN: Can't be bothered to tell her about Michael.
JAMES: There is this thing that's been painted on the wall of the station.
TOBY: What's that?

JAMES, TOBY and MATT stop and stare at it.

MATT: It's a swordfish.
TOBY: Yeah, Matt, I can see that but …
JAMES: It's amazing.
MATT: So big and mad and …
TOBY: Its tail knocking at a window and its sword reaching up to the sky.
MATT: Someone must have done it last night.
TOBY: In the rain?
MATT: Well, it wasn't there yesterday, was it, Tobes?

They look at one another.

HENRY: Nobody in the boarding house mentions Michael, all the talk's about it the latest nudie run. Then there's a fight over showers that ends with blood in the basin and the usual race as the Housemaster yells at us. And Mum calls again from Singapore. Photo of her face stares at me from the screen. All the clothes I brought here used to smell like home. They don't anymore and I don't answer her call.

    HENRY *goes to school.*

TRISTAN: Media out the front of the school.
KIERAN: Some bucktoothed girl with a 2GB mic.
TRISTAN: Channel Seven,
KIERAN: The ABC,
JAMES: This blond reporter / smiles at Sam.
SAM: / Smiles at me.
JAMES: Tells us / I'm an old boy.
KIERAN: / *I'm an old boy.*
SAM: Yeah? What year?
KIERAN: *What do you know about the missing boy?*
TOBY: See Sam and James talking to the reporter.
MATT: They're staring into a camera and / then—
TOBY: / Harley's coming!
MATT: He looks mad!
TOBY: Harley waving his arms around saying:
MATT: *Go inside!*

    Don't speak to the media. If you have something to say you can tell me or put it in the box or—

    Go and sit outside my office right now and wait, you two.

JAMES: Thanks, Sam!
SAM: What?
JAMES: That was your idea.

    JAMES *and* SAM *exit.*

TOBY: Ibis on the field scratches at the grass. Looks up and watches us go. Weird birds.
MATT: Yeah.
TOBY: Looks like Shannon.
MATT: What?
TOBY: The nose and eyes.
MATT: Fuck off! Keep your thoughts to yourself, asshole.
TOBY: Well, she does!

    MATT *leaves, and* TOBY *eventually follows.*

GLEN: Year meeting, period one.
TRISTAN: Sergeant stares.
GLEN: Gannon stares.
TRISTAN: McAlpine stares.
GLEN: Everyone stares back real quiet.
KIERAN: What are they waiting for?
TRISTAN: They're burning holes in our foreheads. Don't let them make eye contact or we'll go blind.
MATT: Finally Gannon tells us that boys will be taken out of class today.
KIERAN: They're talking to as many boys as they can today. They say:
GLEN: *Do not speak to the media.*
TOBY: *This is a delicate matter.*
TRISTAN: *For his family.*
KIERAN: *For the school, schools need to keep boys safe.*
    It sounds like a threat. The way Sergeant tells us not to talk to anyone. Did that feel like a threat?
JAMES: And we sit and wait for Harley. The ibis stares at me through the window as it scratches at a bin. Maybe it knows everything. It has seen and heard everything since the day we first came. That strange-looking thing probably has the answers they need and some they don't, but nobody is listening to it.
SAM: What do you think its name is?
JAMES: The ibis? Boris.
SAM: Yeah, Boris.
JAMES: Look at him snacking away on the rubbish.
SAM: Good one, Boris.
JAMES: Reckon Harley's forgotten us? I need to get to class.
    Should we just go?
SAM: Do you have anything to tell them?
JAMES: No. Do you?
SAM: Not Harley.
JAMES: What?
SAM: For the media, I could have made it up.
JAMES: But you have nothing to say.
SAM: Have you watched the news? They need eyewitnesses.
JAMES: How can you be an eyewitness to something no-one saw?
SAM: They want a story and the reporter chose me. I'd be better on TV

than some loser like Glen. Imagine him stuttering like a spazzo. I need practice.

JAMES: What for?

SAM: You know. Have you been on TV?

JAMES: Yeah, of course, like every night. No. Have you?

SAM: Not free-to-air. I've uploaded shit and stuff like for the band. / But free-to-air is different, it's fully retro but special …

JAMES: / A kid's gone missing, Sam.

Did you hear what I said?

SAM: Yeah, man.

Pause.

Remember that day Miss said I could be in a boy band?

JAMES: No.

SAM: Yeah. It was like a mufti day for some shit and I wore that long coat and there was still cold days back then and I'm like walking towards her and she sees me and the steam coming from my mouth and she goes: *You could be in a boy band, Sam.*

JAMES: Taking the piss.

SAM: We're doing a video this weekend. For our single.

JAMES: What single?

SAM: Not sure yet. Stan and me have been tossing it up.

JAMES: I bet. Since when does Stan sing?

SAM: He's good. His voice is like Drake's. It's the Islander part of him.

JAMES: Stan isn't Islander.

SAM: I'm saying he's a good singer.

JAMES: Do you toss each other or—?

SAM: Yeah, James, we do. Want to watch?

JAMES: How can you make a video clip when you don't even have the song?

SAM: That's what they do now. You don't know nothing.

JAMES: Anything.

SAM: What? What's wrong with you?

JAMES: All this shit going on.

SAM: Sorry, I have a life.

JAMES: Shut up, man.

SAM: So do you reckon the fish and Michael are related?

JAMES: A big swordfish painted on the wall that high a coincidence?

Right.
SAM: Who did it then?
JAMES: Don't know.
SAM: Do you know him?
JAMES: He's in our classes, Sam.
SAM: But I mean heaps of kids in your class you don't know.
JAMES: He was in our cabin at camp.
SAM: In Year Nine?
JAMES: Spencer spewed in his bag.
SAM: Spencer's feral. Was Michael in *Oliver!*?

> JAMES *nods*.

Was he a Londoner or a workhouse boy?
JAMES: Backstage.
SAM: Oh.
JAMES: He has a tattoo, you know.
SAM: What?
JAMES: A tattoo.
SAM: Bullshit he does.

> JAMES *shrugs*.

What of?
  Where?

> JAMES *points vaguely*.

How do you know that?
JAMES: Saw it changing in PE.
SAM: Why were you looking at him?
JAMES: He was next to me.
SAM: It's probably texta.

> JAMES *shakes his head*.

What is it then?
JAMES: I don't know.
SAM: You saw it, you must. So either it's really shit ink or …
  I bet it's a swordfish? Is it?
  James?

> JAMES *nods*.

How big is it?

JAMES *shows him.*

No. He's like fifteen. How did he get a tattoo?

JAMES *shrugs.*

Does it look like that fish at the station?

JAMES: I don't know, I saw it for a second.

SAM: Wouldn't pick that, hey? He must have good connections or ID. Maybe he has a whole secret life. Maybe he's having some big joke on us. He's hiding and watching and …

JAMES: Find out soon enough.

SAM: I got to get tattoos. Musos need them. Just on my arms and legs. Full sleeves. Not tacky shit. I saw this guy who had a *Lord of the Rings* sleeve theme which was pretty cool. Timeless. Gandalf right up the top of his shoulder staring down at Golem and the hobbits.

Nothing on the neck.

This guy comes into work, he has 'Tracy' [*indicating*] right across here. Man, if I was Tracy and he came home to show me what he'd done to his throat I reckon I might have gone into hiding 'cause that's a lot of pressure.

So when did you talk to Michael?

JAMES: What?

SAM: Tell me.

JAMES: Sometimes at lunch in the Art room.

SAM: Oooh.

JAMES: Fuck off. It's quiet in there you get shit done.

SAM: Is that where he showed you his tattoo?

JAMES *rolls his eyes.*

JAMES: At least I'm not stroking Stan!

SAM: Maybe you should tell Harley about all this. The tattoo and …

JAMES: What?—

SAM: Here he comes. Tell him now.

They both watch as Harley enters and approaches.

TOBY: We get pulled out of class one by one.

KIERAN: Matt.

TOBY: Like fish pulled through a hole in the ice.

GLEN: Kieran.
TOBY: They line up the fish.
KIERAN: Tristan.
TOBY: Like an Eskimo fish market.
HENRY: Glen.
TOBY: Sparkling scales and glazed-over eyes.
HENRY: Kieran.
SAM: Harley stares at us and asks if we have anything to say.

    I don't. So I go.

JAMES: And I'm there alone with Harley. I want to help but I don't know what to say so I just look at Harley's whiskers and the hair on his hands and the papers on his desk and the photo of him and his wife and his sons who used to come to school here a couple of years back. He looks at the photo too. Wonder if he's thinking the same thing as me. Can I go now, sir?

    TOBY *stares at the ibis.*

His name's Boris.
TOBY: Yeah?
JAMES: He sees everything, you know.

Ashutosh Bidkar (left) as Henry and Louis Nicholls as James in Newington College's 2016 production. (Photo: Christopher Hayles)

TOBY: Yeah?

They've called me in.

TOBY *and* JAMES *watch the ibis for a moment.*

We hear the strange squawking noise. Or flapping.

JAMES *goes.*

SAM *picks up his guitar and plucks at the strings again.*

He's writing a song in his head.

He tries to add MICHAEL*'s name to the tune and gives up and goes.* MICHAEL *appears.*

KIERAN *places something in the coward's box while* MICHAEL *watches on. The bell rings.*

Michael lives near Matt and me. We never hung out with him. Matt and me have this hide-out like a kind of cubbyhouse.

Last year we thought that someone was staying in it overnight. They didn't make a mess or anything so we just figured that whoever it was needed a place to stay.

And there was this day when we'd hung out in the afternoon and it was getting dark and we were going home and there was someone in the bush. Someone was there and they were walking towards the hide-out and I said to Matt it's probably the dude who stays here at night, so we left but Matt watched from his house and he saw this guy who he thought / was—

MATT: / You told them that?

TOBY: Yeah.

MATT: I don't know if that was Michael.

TOBY: No. But you said probably.

MATT: Yeah but—

TOBY: And if he did stay there. If he was staying there, then …

MATT: What?

TOBY: We have to tell them. If he was sleeping rough there could have been trouble at home or something.

MATT: You're a dick.

TOBY: It might be information that they need, that's all.

MATT: We don't even know if it was him.

TOBY: But—

MATT: What about the stuff we did there?
TOBY: What? We drunk a few beers there and smoked a / bit of pot. They aren't going to go and check on it.
MATT: I wish you told me you were going to tell, man. It's like fifty metres away from my house. If my parents get involved ... you know what my mum's like.

> MATT *leaves* TOBY.

TRISTAN: Sergeant, the school counsellor and Kelly Clarkson sit in a row.
KIERAN: Like an interview for parole.
TRISTAN: Or a talk show.
KIERAN: Like 'Entertainment Tonight'.
TRISTAN: Like *Q&A* with a live audience.
KIERAN: I'm on it.
TRISTAN: Questions prepared. Half of them gunning for Michael, the other half ...
KIERAN: Did I know Michael?
TRISTAN: Through cadets. / We were in the same platoon.
KIERAN: / We were in the same platoon.
TRISTAN: But that's it.
KIERAN: We spoke a couple of times but—
TRISTAN: I never spoke to him more than giving him orders.
KIERAN: At think-out?
TRISTAN: He's just not my type of guy I guess.
KIERAN: At think-out?
TRISTAN: At think-out? I don't know.
KIERAN: Well ... yeah something happened.
TRISTAN: What happens at think-out stays at think-out.
KIERAN: It'd stuff me up to tell.
TRISTAN: You know, it stays in the bush.
KIERAN: I mean if people find out about this.

> KIERAN *waits for* TRISTAN *to leave.*
>
> *When* TRISTAN *is gone ...*

Okay. On the first night, we'd just started think-out and were all in our sites. I set up my cover and my water and I do my knots like seven hundred times and then ... I thought it was going to be fine, thought the last person who'd be chicken-shit is me, and I'm sitting out there and the time is passing really slow and I know I can't go to sleep yet 'cause it's probably only eight o'clock and I don't want to wake up in the middle of the night and be stuck awake forever in the dark. It's really black out there. I'm feeling a bit … start thinking stuff that worries me. Dumb stuff but …

I'm thinking about all the things I've shot on screen. The zombies and … They've all come back to life again and they're on a convergence mission. They're moving towards me to get revenge. It's funny at first and then I realise it isn't funny sitting there in the black alone, those thoughts aren't that much fun. I realise I haven't got anything to defend myself except a knife and fork and the knot rope. And I know the zombies have an arsenal and I kind of work myself up and I know it makes no sense but it's pinging around in my head and I can't stay in the dark alone so I walk. I sneak to the nearest site just to see someone, you can't tell this. 'Cause we aren't meant to and if they find out now like … But I was scared.

So anyhow I kind of crawled in the dark to the next site and Michael's there. He has the next site. He's made a little fire even though it isn't allowed and his hands are covered in blood and he's watching this hunk of meat cooking on the flame. *How the hell did you get meat?*

It smells good 'cause all I've eaten is dried-up rations and I'm starving. Michael smiles and spreads out his tarp and motions to sit with his blood-caked hands. He doesn't talk, nobody can talk—it's think-out—so we sit there quiet as, we just watch the fire. And in the end I have to ask: *What is it? What have you killed?* Lip reading, you know, and then he re-enacts how he killed this possum and it's the funniest thing I've ever seen, I tell you and we sit there hungry as hell but not sure we can eat the possum and then my gut growls and I grab a possum leg and he grabs one too and we eat possum and it tastes like lamb but bitter and stringy and then in the distance there's some kid singing 'She's Got a Fast Car' at the top of his voice which gives me cover to sneak back.

    SAM *plays more of the song.*

TRISTAN: Strikes me as weird that some kid can just vanish.
HENRY: Nobody asks me about Michael.
TRISTAN: When you think of all the ways you can track someone.

HENRY: I don't get called down 'cause I'm the new kid.
TRISTAN: All the cameras everywhere.
HENRY: No questions. No-one even gets where I'm from.
TRISTAN: Surveillance.
HENRY: I'm the new kid from Singapore.
TRISTAN: I'm willing to tell them if it comes up.
HENRY: But I know him. I know Michael.
TRISTAN: They cross-examine us all but don't have right questions.
HENRY: The day after I arrive here everything's still strange. I'm hungry because the boarding house food takes getting used to. Michael takes me for potato scallops after class. We eat them together and hang out. He shows me his tag in the tunnel up under the train tracks. He does it late at night when nobody else is out. Michael tells me how to get back into the boarding house if I'm out late at night, if I misjudge the time and they lock the boarding house up, he says you can set off the alarm and slip in to the line of boys waiting for the firemen to give the okay. Nobody suspects. He doesn't board there now.
TRISTAN: They didn't ask me the right stuff so I didn't say.
HENRY: And he is different. The way he sees things. Some of the things he sees. / Some kids are different. They stand out.
TRISTAN: / Some kids are different. They stand out.
HENRY: See how some of them treated him.
TRISTAN: Some kids ask for it. Stand out in ways that make them easy prey.
HENRY: Kids say stuff to him. Call him / freak, sissy. Fag.
TRISTAN: / Freak, sissy. Fag. Just a bit of fun.
HENRY: Last week Tristan comes up behind Michael and puts his arm around his neck and kind of spins him around and he falls onto the ground. I didn't know what to do when he said, / 'You little sissy bitch'.
TRISTAN: / You little sissy bitch. Don't make trouble for yourself, Swordfish, or your life'll be a fucking misery.
HENRY: Then Tristan left and it was just us and I didn't know what to say.
TRISTAN: / Stare at Kelly Clarkson and wish I had something more to tell.
GLEN: / Stare at Kelly Clarkson and wish I had something more to tell.

    I want to say there is something but can I share it with you in private. Kelly Clarkson'll understand. She'll wink and take my hand and lead me up to her office and open the door, she'll say that because this is a special case we should shut the door. It's hot in the room with the door shut, it's actually really hot so I take off my jumper and she smiles at me as she takes off her jacket. She unbuttons her shirt she smiles, she smells good. Kelly says you don't have to stand all the way over there. Relax and come and sit here and she giggles a bit and I see she's wearing red high heels and she reaches out and holds my hand and whispers: *I'm so glad we trust each other like this, you know whatever happens in here stays in here.*

HENRY: Sissy, faggot, fag. Same dull words as anywhere.

    HENRY *thinks about this, then exits.*

SAM: Thursday night. I've got a job at a fruit shop. Just up the road from the school. Dezzy is on tonight. My first girlfriend was called Ming. Dad called her the vase which sucked after we broke it off. Been single for a while which is probably good 'cause I'm in a band and a lot of musos are players, you know.

    Dezzy is short for Desdemona I guess, like in that boring play we're doing with Petrie.

    Hey, Dezzy, where's Steve?

DEZZY: *Not here.*

SAM: Steve's the boss. He's also Dezzy's uncle.

    What's Dezzy short for?

DEZZY: *Despina.*

SAM: Oh, right. 'Cause we're doing this play and …

DEZZY: *What?*

SAM: Dezzy's older than me. She works the checkout and wears these tops that look like she has covered two melons in cotton just here.

    An awkward moment when DEZZY *notices* SAM *watching her.*

    How's uni, Dezzy?

DEZZY: *Hate it. It's full of stuck-up cows who don't have to work to pay fees.*

SAM: We aren't going out but I imagine we are.

    I reckon Dezzy does too. I catch her looking at me from the registers while I unpack peaches.

DEZZY: *Steve said do the plums as well.*

SAM: Is he gonna come back?

DEZZY: *Yeah. He has to lock up.*

SAM: I imagine what we'd do if Steve didn't come back. If it was just us two here at closing time.

DEZZY: *You dropped one.*

SAM: All the berries, put in the fridges. The cabbage leaves swept away. Floors clean and boxes folded up, nobody else here …

DEZZY: *Steve's back. He's parking. Did you deal with those rotten cauliflowers?*

SAM: You going to go to that party Saturday?

DEZZY: *Don't know.*

SAM: Me neither. Kid at our school went missing.

DEZZY: *Saw it on the news.*

SAM: What station?

    DEZZY *shrugs.*

Just … thought you might have seen me on ABC.

DEZZY: *No.*

SAM: So anyway, Mum and Dad are being a bit cautious.

DEZZY: *You're not allowed to go?*

SAM: Working on it.

DEZZY: *Because of …*

SAM: Michael. You know I've never said anyone's name so many times in one week.

DEZZY: *So he's your mate?*

    It occurs to SAM *that there is mileage in this. He nods.*

They say there might be a kidnapper on the loose.

SAM: Mum's worried and shit.

DEZZY: *Not as worried as mine. She spends her life saying she wishes she'd never brought us into the world with all the bombings and shit. Know what I think?*

SAM: No.

DEZZY: *One kid at your school is really pretty minor in the scheme of it all, you know. Does your mum watch the news?*

SAM: I think it's different when it happens close to home.

DEZZY: *Yeah? Why?*

SAM: Just, vicinity.

DEZZY: *So what do they reckon happened to him?*

SAM: No-one knows.

DEZZY: *People don't just disappear, you know.*
SAM: They do.
DEZZY: *What are they doing to find him?*
SAM: School's interviewing us all and there is a cop.
DEZZY: *I meant what are you and all the kids in the year doing?*

    DEZZY's *question hits* SAM *like a slap.*

TOBY: Michael's fifth night out.
MATT: Yeah.
TOBY: Did you check the cubbyhouse?
MATT: Yeah. There's nothing.
TOBY: Did you actually look?
MATT: Yeah.
TOBY: 'Cause I could come over tomorrow …
MATT: Thing is …
TOBY: Or on the weekend? I haven't been over for ages.
MATT: Can't.
TOBY: Why? Is this about the ibis comment?
MATT: No. I'm just really busy, man.
TOBY: Is it …?
MATT: Look, it's not you. It's / Shannon.
TOBY: / Shannon.
MATT: She has stuff going on and …
TOBY: You're not married to her, Matt.
MATT: I know that, Toby.
TOBY: Well, you aren't, you know.
MATT: Yeah, thanks.
TOBY: We used to hang out and since you started going out …
MATT: Yeah … well.
TOBY: I know what you do in the cubbyhouse, Matt.
MATT: / Shut up.
TOBY: / With Shannon.
MATT: How?
TOBY: It's just obvious. Don't know why you've gone all weird about it. If I had a girlfriend I'd take her there too.
MATT: But you don't.
TOBY: Yeah, thanks, I know. Is that why you don't want your mum to know?

MATT *nods*.

'Cause she'd go in and check and—
MATT: Yeah, so thanks, Tobes.
TOBY: Did you take those pics down?
MATT: Yeah. Shannon's kind of redecorated. Just a rug and—
TOBY: You turned our cubby into a shag shack!
MATT: Not yet I haven't. Candy keeps coming in at the wrong time. Wagging her tail and sniffing. She knocked over these cups Shannon brought over and they smashed. It ruined the moment.

MATT *and* TOBY *laugh*.

JAMES: Mum and Dad are out. Sit in my room at my desk and stare out the window.

I can see straight into Charlie's bedroom from mine. Which would be weird if you just moved in, but it's always been that way.

Me and Charlie, we're the same age. We used to hang out a lot. We're still friendly but he went to the school down the road and his friends are all like into music and drama and mine aren't. He painted the walls of his room black. Mum made me keep mine white.

I can see Charlie's bed and his desk and the posters on his wall when the blinds are open. Kids who come over say bet you wish Charlie was a girl.

GLEN: I google Kelly Clarkson. Not my Kelly. The famous one. Turns out Sam knows shit. Kelly Clarkson's not a porn star. Mum knows who she is. She says she has her CDs. She digs one out for me to play but it's not in the case.

JAMES: I see Charlie sitting out the back smoking a cigarette and all I think is I didn't know he smokes. He's wearing a hood and his skin is white in the moonlight and he looks like a kid in a film, not the kid next door. Blowing the smoke in and out. He doesn't see me.

Charlie's the only one who knows except … It's a bit weird between us even though he says it's cool.

MICHAEL *appears for a moment*.

Just Charlie and Michael know.

JAMES *looks in* MICHAEL*'s direction, but he's gone*.

GLEN: Get to school early Friday. It's the last day of term.

Go in to see if Kelly's there. Might tell her mum's a fan.
Walk up the steps to the—
PERCIVAL: *You're early, Glen.*
GLEN: Mr Percival, yeah guess so, yeah.
PERCIVAL: *Can I help with something?*
GLEN: I'm looking for the cop. Kelly Clarkson.
PERCIVAL: *I don't think she's back today.*
GLEN: But … Her desk and chair are there.
PERCIVAL: / *Yeah, but she's gone back to the station.*
GLEN: / The ones that she takes outside when it's sunny.
PERCIVAL: *Yeah, I know the ones you mean, Glen.*

    Pause.

GLEN: When is she coming back?
PERCIVAL: *I think she's done here, mate.*
GLEN: Oh.
PERCIVAL: *What?*
    You alright?
GLEN: Yeah … just.
PERCIVAL: *Did you have something to say? Are you a mate of Michael's?*
GLEN: —
PERCIVAL: *Did you want me to pass on something?*
GLEN: It's alright.
PERCIVAL: *Fine. Well, if you need to talk, I'm here.*
GLEN: Thanks, sir.
PERCIVAL: *So tell me. How's that brother of yours doing?*

    GLEN *shrugs.*

Can you do me a favour, mate? Take that cop's desk and chair back to my room?

    GLEN *is disappointed.*

JAMES: Friday morning PE change rooms Tristan's changing …
TRISTAN: What are you looking at?
JAMES: What's that? That thing round your neck.

    TRISTAN *shrugs.*

Where's it from?
TRISTAN: Found it.

JAMES: Where?
TRISTAN: Outside the school on the street, I don't know.
JAMES: When?
TRISTAN: I don't know. What is this?
JAMES: It's not yours.
TRISTAN: Didn't say it was. I said found it.
JAMES: Just it isn't yours and I know whose it is and …
TRISTAN: What, James?

> TRISTAN *stares menacingly at* JAMES. *He laughs in* JAMES' *face, then exits.*
>
> MATT *places something in the coward's box.*
>
> *The bell rings.*

HENRY: Assembly.
KIERAN: Assembly period two.
TOBY: Harley up the front.
TRISTAN: No cops this time, teachers stand in their place.
KIERAN: But there's something strange. First assembly since …
HENRY: With so much to be said.
KIERAN: Nobody knows where to start.
MATT: So many things we've been told not to say.
KIERAN: Nobody knows what we can.
TOBY: Can we talk about the fish at the station?
MATT: Will they tell us what Clarkson's been told?
KIERAN: What's been written and put inside the box.
TRISTAN: News from the outside.
GLEN: A call from a witness.
TOBY: A demand from kidnappers.
KIERAN: Or a photo of a boy in a balaclava.
TOBY: A ransom note with cut-out letters from Michael Swordfish.
TRISTAN: Box with his cut-off finger inside.
KIERAN: Harley puts his hand up, he doesn't need to say a word.
TRISTAN: Then there's a woman in green on the stage.
JAMES: It's Michael's mum.
GLEN: How do you know?
KIERAN: Harley said it's Mrs Swordfish.
GLEN: She's much hotter than my mum.
SAM: Yeah.

GLEN: Don't diss my mum.
TOBY: She smiles at us all.
GLEN: What's she going to say?
KIERAN: Why is she smiling?
TRISTAN: Maybe Michael was a dickhead at home and she's glad he's gone.
KIERAN: Maybe she did it.
TOBY: Did what?
KIERAN: Arranged a disappearance like …
TOBY: Kieran, that's sick, man.
JAMES: Maybe he's been found.
SAM: He'd be here if they'd found him.
JAMES: I guess.
MATT: She stares at us for ages.
GLEN: Then she speaks softly, doesn't say much.
KIERAN: She says she's grateful for our help.
TRISTAN: She's glad that her son goes to such a good school.
HENRY: Then …
MATT: She stares out at us all.
KIERAN: She looks around the hall.
TOBY: Her eyes fix on an empty chair down the end of our row and that sets her off.
JAMES: And she cries while Mr Harley tells us to: / *Think very hard.*
HENRY: / *Think very hard. If there is anything that you have not reported, anything at all no matter how silly or insignificant you think it might be, tell someone, doesn't matter who.* / *Or put it in the box outside the canteen.*
GLEN: / Or put it in the box outside the canteen.
TRISTAN: Put it in the coward box.
MATT: Harley leads Mrs Swordfish away and then Sergeant comes out and tells all of us to have a safe holiday.
JAMES: Do you remember with Mitchell Strong?
TOBY: We got the whole day out of class and there was that service.
JAMES: Some kids took the whole week off.
TOBY: Everyone brought in photos.
JAMES: And flowers.
TOBY: Remember the rugby team walking through the school with bouquets of flowers?

JAMES: Bunches stacked around the entrance to the Year Twelve common room.
TOBY: A sea of flowers.
JAMES: School should have looked beautiful but it looked strange instead.

They leave and TRISTAN *is alone.*

TRISTAN *waits and when nobody is looking he opens the information box, takes all the papers out and goes.*

SAM: Note comes around in period five.
TOBY: Miss says:
MISS: *Fold it and put it away and give it to your parents and—*
JAMES: Miss looks at the note and her face drops.
MATT: I think the worst.
SAM: Is it about—?
JAMES: And then I see it. I see what Miss sees.
MATT: The heading on the note …
TOBY: The name on the note.
TRISTAN: Michelle Swordfish.

TRISTAN *laughs.*

KIERAN: Ha! No!
JAMES: You can hear it being whispered across the school.
SAM / TRISTAN: Michelle!
JAMES: You can hear it downstairs as one of the Year Seven boys reads it and points it out.
MATT: Doberman didn't proofread.
KIERAN: Kids pissing themselves across the school.
TRISTAN: Some comic relief at last.
JAMES: You can't let them send this out, Miss. You can't let them send this home.
MISS: *It's an unfortunate typo, James, but ...*
JAMES: But what?
TRISTAN: Here we go.
JAMES: It is not just a typo, Miss, don't you see?
MISS: *Yes, but what do you want me to do, James?*
JAMES: Send them all back. Take everyone of these back and get rid of them / for his sake.

TRISTAN: / And the nominees for best drama are …
James Graham in *The Typo*.
JAMES: Fuck off.
MISS: / *Language, James!*
JAMES: / This is for Michael's sake.
TRISTAN: Glen Simmons for *The Retard Strikes Back*.
JAMES: *Fuck you!* You think this is funny?
TRISTAN: Michelle Swordfish for *The Vanishing*.
JAMES: What did you say you—?
MISS: *Final warning! Both of you settle down and sit. Now! Now! I can't take the note back, James.*
JAMES: Why not?
MISS: *Think of all the paper.*
JAMES: I don't care about all the paper.
Don't you see, Miss? As if all this isn't enough. If he comes back—
MISS: *He will come back.*
JAMES: Then when he comes back do you think this typo will die? Do you think the kids out there will forget it? We don't even know where he went or why, but if he comes back, the least we can do …
TRISTAN: We can send Michelle to Ladies' College.
HENRY: And that's when James cries in class.
MISS: *Go and get a drink of water, James. The rest of you, scribble out Michelle and write Michael.*

Bell rings.

Have a safe holiday, everyone.

They all leave, except TRISTAN *and* JAMES.

JAMES: What do you want?
TRISTAN: You okay?
JAMES: As if you care.
TRISTAN: You were really upset in class, mate.
JAMES: Save it.
TRISTAN: I don't know what your problem is, man. Except you're acting like my sister on her period. What is wrong with you? Who cares if his name's spelt wrong?
JAMES: I said what do you want?
TRISTAN: I thought I'd give you this.

TRISTAN *holds out the talisman.*

JAMES: Why do you have it?

TRISTAN: I told you, I found it.

JAMES: When?

TRISTAN: Last week. Held on to it. I was going to give it back to him but he went and vanished on us and so I thought …

JAMES: What?

TRISTAN: Seeing you miss him so much you might want to mind it. Or if he doesn't come back, keep it.

JAMES *stares at the talisman.* TRISTAN *laughs softly.*

Would that upset you if he didn't come back? Would this bring you some comfort?

JAMES: You're sick in the head, man.

TRISTAN: Thanks, mate. You know I don't know if I'd recognise him out in the street. Would you? What's he look like, James? What colour are his eyes?

JAMES: They're green.

TRISTAN: There you go.

He blows JAMES *a kiss.*

JAMES *does not take the talisman.*

Take it!

JAMES *shakes his head.*

Sure you don't want it?

JAMES: Yes.

TRISTAN: I thought you would. That you might like to take it home and hold it and cry yourself to sleep on your bed.

JAMES: Fuck you.

TRISTAN: Never took you for a fag. Crying over poor Michelle.

JAMES: Fuck you! It's Michael!

TRISTAN *stares at* JAMES *and gives him a last chance to take the talisman.*

TRISTAN: Don't want it?

JAMES: No. You figure out what to do with it.

JAMES *goes.*

TRISTAN: What kind of loser doesn't have a Facebook? I set one up. For Michael. Michelle. For fun. 'Cause I'm bored and it's the start of the holidays. Could do check-ins all over the place and mess with the investigation. Or …

> TRISTAN *has an idea.*
>
> SAM *plays.*
>
> *An interlude where each of the boys watches a different screen.*

JAMES: Mum cooks all day for a dinner party and I stay in my room watching for Charlie, want to see him. I want to go over and tell him what's been going on. Sit on his bed and tell him about what happened in the Art room that day between Michael and me. Don't know who to tell, need to tell someone about the Art room and also about that there was this night when I was here in my room and Michael called. I didn't even know he had my number.

> MICHAEL *appears.*

Where are you?

MICHAEL: I'm in my room lying on my bed.

JAMES: I'm on my bed too.

MICHAEL: Lying down?

JAMES: Yeah.

MICHAEL: Same. Under the covers or on top?

JAMES: On top.

> We talk for ages. Michael tells me about his favourite place. This place they used to go to down the coast when he was a kid.

MICHAEL: We used to go fishing. We'd pull in these dumb little bream, the same ones over and over again, little tears on the mouths from the hooks that came before. I never knew fish were so …

JAMES: What?

MICHAEL: What's your favourite place, James?

JAMES: I don't know.

MICHAEL: Go on. Just …

JAMES: I like it when we go to the Art room.

MICHAEL: Yeah. It's cool, hey.

> *Pause.*

Hey, listen to this.

MICHAEL *puts on a song on the other end of the phone.*

JAMES: I lay back on my bed and close my eyes and listen. We listen to the whole song and I want it to go forever, knowing that he is on his bed doing the same thing.

MICHAEL *goes and* JAMES *feels alone.*

I want to ask Charlie if he thinks I should tell. Will telling them that help? Do I have a right to say? I mean at school they say it's fine but it isn't that simple and I can't just put it in the coward's box. Not that. I have to do something.

MATT: Holidays and I see Shannon heaps. She makes lots of plans for us. Shannon is really pretty and I love a lot of things about her.

Yeah, I mean love.

Her hair.

JAMES: The way he smells. Kind of peppery, can't tell them that.

MATT: Shannon's smell. It's kind of sweet and when I get close to her it makes me feel like I am some weird insect that can't stay away from her.

/ I love her lips.

JAMES: / I like his lips.

MATT: They're soft and full and pink and I love love love love love love her lips. I mean they drive me totally mad, I just want to like do this all day. Her ears are like little shells you'd find on a beach in Barbados.

JAMES: / It isn't just …

MATT: / It isn't just physical.

Frustrated, JAMES *leaves.*

I love being seen out with her and I love the way she says my name and the nicknames she calls me which are kind of between us so I won't say them. I love the look she gets on her face when she's concentrating, but this is the problem. That look … it never stays for long. Because Shannon has to look at her phone. So she will try something for about ten seconds before she stops and has to check her phone.

GLEN: First weekend of the holidays, I'm at this party with Sam.

There aren't many guys here, mate.

SAM: That's a good thing, man.

GLEN: Yeah, I know that.

SAM: 'Cause you hang out with guys all week, Glen.
GLEN: Yeah, I know that.
SAM: Just watch your mouth.
GLEN: What do you mean?
SAM: Just don't say stupid shit like you do in class. Like, just think. Before. You. Speak. You want a beer?

> GLEN *thinks*.

GLEN: Yes.
SAM: Good one.
GLEN: What is this?
SAM: Aldi shit. Gets you there though. Drink it.
GLEN: We watch some of the girls smoking and dancing to R&B.
> Where are these chicks from?

> SAM *grins*.

SAM: Does it matter?
GLEN: Alright!

> SAM *sees* DEZZY *arrive*.

Who's that? Why've you gone all weird?
SAM: That's Dezzy, man. Back in a minute.
GLEN: But …
SAM: What, Glen?
> Mingle!
MATT: Shannon is like addicted to her phone. And because I spend so much time with her, it means I've enabled her addiction, become addicted to it too. But tonight I'm sick of the feed about Michael. All the rumours and the likes and the shares. I just want to turn it all off. I try to tell Shannon this when we meet, I ask like do you really need to be on your phone right now and she kind of laughs and rolls her eyes and says: *No, Dad.*

And we are sitting on the train and I say why don't you put it down and *watch*. Make a list.

An anorexic girl.

A guy with acne.

An Agatha Christie novel left on a seat.

The sad face scratched on the wall of the train.

We walk along George Street.

A ribbon in the gutter.

Get off your phone, Shan, and make a list like mine.

The things I saw when I wasn't looking at my phone. Because I've been thinking of all the things we might have missed if we had've put our phones in our pockets.

Shannon tries. You can tell she is really trying. But I think it is actually really hurting her, like giving her physical pain and she can't put the phone away for long enough to listen to my list let alone make her own.

GLEN: I stand there looking at the space Sam's left. The space between me and the rest of the party. I'm heading home when this girl smiles at me.

JULIA: *Hey.*

GLEN: Hey.

JULIA: *You look like you've lost your best friend.*

GLEN: Um ... no. He's over there.

JULIA: *The rock star guy?*

GLEN: Um ...

JULIA: *I'm Julia.*

MATT: I'm carrying this stupid bucket of popcorn Shannon made me get which cost twelve bucks. The cinema's is full and we're late so we have sit up the front, the screen is like right in our faces, you can smell the actors' breath and I hate that because of what it does to your neck. The movie takes forever to start and Shannon keeps checking her phone as she shoves popcorn into her mouth. I don't eat any of it to see how much Shannon will get through. The previews go on and on and everyone around me is playing with their phones and the movie starts and she puts her phone on silent and has eaten maybe three kilograms of popcorn. Five minutes later all the popcorn's gone and I know the movie's gonna suck. It is a remake of some film that sucked in the first place.

GLEN: So what subjects do you do at school?

JULIA: *What?*

TRISTAN: I read through everything in the box and decide to do a little WikiLeaks, a Panama job ... I'll upload the things boys wrote one by one, word for word. Every secret, every scrawl about Swordfish. And then I'll post it all online.

GLEN: Hobbies? Do you have hobbies?
JULIA: *Like? Yeah. I guess so. I play netball. I like baking.*
GLEN: Like cakes?
JULIA: *Fruit loaves and muffins and stuff.*
GLEN: Right. Yum.
MATT: The movie finishes and the phones come back out and as we walk out Shannon is sending a message to someone as she's repeating one of the lines that Jennifer Lawrence said and then she puts her phone in her pocket and waits.

Finally. Finally she's put her phone away.

Then she just looks at me and asks:
SHANNON: *Do you have something you want to say to me?*
MATT: What?
SHANNON: *This isn't working for me, Matt.*
MATT: Huh?
TRISTAN: Coward box confessions. Post one.
MATT: We are there in the cinema foyer on a Saturday night surrounded by boyfriends and girlfriends.
SHANNON: *I want to break it off with you.*
MATT: It is the most undramatic breakup. Shannon doesn't even cry. As she gets her phone back out she says:
SHANNON: *Expressing myself is the most important thing to me. Why do you want to take that away from me? I already have a dad.*
TRISTAN: Coward confession. Post two.
JAMES: When I go downstairs Cassie's in the kitchen drinking something dark green and this is weird—
CASSIE: *What?*
JAMES: You're never home.
CASSIE: *No!*
JAMES: For the first time in like five years Cassie is in my room, she crashes onto my bed and reaches out and ruffles my hair.
CASSIE: *What's going on, little bro?*
JAMES: Are you on drugs?
CASSIE: *No. Just asking what's going on.*
JAMES: Just shit.
CASSIE: *What shit?*

    JAMES *is about to tell her but her phone sounds.*

Sorry. I have to get this.

TRISTAN: Coward box. Post three.

KIERAN: Level six and the landline rings, I can't can't can't get it—
Dad? Are you there? Can you get that?

TRISTAN: Post four. A sad one. Wonder who wrote that?

KIERAN: Phone rings again. I'm on a level seven rampage kill can't kill can't kill can't kill can't can't answer …
Fuck! Thanks for that, Dad, hello?
What?
Online?
Are you kidding? The comments from that box? No?!
Who would do that?

TRISTAN: Coward post five.

GLEN: Julia has a really nice laugh and I don't say the first thing that comes into my head, I kind of wait and do this … and I can tell Julia thinks I'm pretty smart, like I'm a thinker.
There's chemistry between us.

JULIA *smiles and laughs.*

JULIA: *I heard your friend saying that someone you know has gone missing.*

GLEN: Yeah.

JULIA: *Like someone really close to him.*

GLEN: Yeah. Kind of.

TRISTAN: Post six.

JULIA: *That must be hard on him.*
What's his name?

GLEN: The guy who went missing?

JULIA: *No, your friend.*

TRISTAN: Seven.

GLEN: Sam.

JULIA: *He's cute.*

TRISTAN: Eight.

GLEN: Do you think?

TRISTAN: Nine.

JULIA: *Does he have a girlfriend?*

GLEN: Yeah.

JULIA: *Oh. So, what I don't get is what are you two doing here?*
GLEN: What do you mean?
JULIA: *If you're really close to this guy why aren't you doing something to help find him?*
TRISTAN: Post ten. Eleven.
GLEN: Like what? But then a fight breaks out.
SAM: Between this dude with black hair and an angry guy.
JULIA: *Broken bottles, glass everywhere and blood.*
SAM: And we just stand there and watch.
GLEN: Watch one guy beat another one up.
SAM: Thud.
GLEN: Thud.
SAM: Thud.
GLEN: Thud.
TRISTAN: Post twelve.
SAM: Music dies and a pot plant gets smashed.
GLEN: The party's over.
SAM: That guy was beaten up really bad.
GLEN: The blood drips like custard down his pudding face and we just …
JULIA: *You guys could have done something.*
GLEN: Watch it all.
SAM: What were we meant to do?
JULIA: *Stop them fighting, you losers. I'm out of here.*
GLEN: Wait. Can I get your number?
SAM: She's gone.
GLEN: Yeah.
SAM: Did you kiss her?
GLEN: No, I didn't kiss her. The fight broke out just after she asked me why were at the party, why we weren't doing something to help find Michael.
SAM: Tough luck. It's not our job to find Michael.
GLEN: Whose job is it?

And I don't know what gets into me but I run. I run and I want to smash bins over and scream.
SAM: Glen! Stop it, man. Glen! Stop!

    GLEN *screams and pushes the chairs over.*

SAM *joins him in destroying the set.*

They collapse and sit and stare into space.

TRISTAN: Finish the posts. Everything is online.

KIERAN: Someone's set it up. And he's loaded data. Comments from us, from the boys from the school, one by one. Who would do that?

HENRY: Wait until it gets dark. Grab my backpack and go.

HENRY *paints a huge swordfish on the wall.*

I paint one on the wall near the bus stop. One on the shop by the school. One on the wall of the hall and …

JAMES: I go to where he lives. To find the corner where he was sitting when he was last seen. There's a cop car with a cop sitting inside on his phone. And on the corner there's a dummy dressed in our school uniform. The dummy is Michael's size and he's sitting in the gutter holding a fake phone. And behind him wired to the fence is a sign that says: 'Have you seen this boy?'

GLEN *looks at* SAM.

SAM: Glen? You okay, man?

Glen.

GLEN *shakes his head and sobs.*

SAM *goes and to him. He reaches out to comfort him but doesn't quite know how.*

JAMES: Cop doesn't notice me as I pass. So I go to Michael's house, creep up the side of the house. Nobody home. I check the windows and look for signs. I don't know what I expect to find. The house is a mess. Nobody's washed up and there is stuff in piles everywhere. I find Michael's room. It's tidier than the rest. His clothes folded up in a pile and his bed's made. He has the same quilt cover as me.

The books, the clothes, the desk, the bed, the model plane, the pile of games, a little plastic dragon blowing a puff of plastic smoke. A fish tank with nothing in it but water. A drawing he's done and a photo in a photo frame of him and his sister and his mum and dad. They're smiling right at me.

This is the only space that this boy owns. This could be my room. This could be my space. Is this all we are? Him and me? Just tenants taking up space? Are the only people who notice the sadness of this empty room his parents when they walk past it each day? Do they just lock the door in the end so they can keep going?

And then I see it and I know. The photo. The place in the photo, the trees and the road and the path and …

GLEN: I got to get home, Sam.

> GLEN *and* SAM *go*.
>
> HENRY *paints another swordfish while* MICHAEL *appears before* JAMES.

JAMES: His favourite place. And I remember what he said to me in the Art room.

> JAMES *and* MICHAEL *come face to face.*

MICHAEL: I knew you'd come.

JAMES: How?

MICHAEL: I don't know, just did. I guess I hoped you would.

I saw you watching me through the window.

JAMES: I saw you too.

> *Pause.*

MICHAEL: Come here.

JAMES: Why?

MICHAEL: Can you hold me? I don't know if I want to do anything else right now but. Can you just …?

> JAMES *goes to him.*
>
> *They hold one another until* JAMES *lets go.*

JAMES: You're cold.

MICHAEL: I know. Just …

JAMES: What's going on, Michael?

MICHAEL: I saw this kid outside the school this morning. Kid from the prep school sitting next to his dad on a fence. They looked so alike, it's kind of weird like seeing a father ape and his son in the zoo.

The dad was sad and he was staring into space.

And the boy is watching his dad. He seems to know what the sadness is. He kind of reaches up and tries to put his little arm around his dad but the dad turns and looks at his son and shakes his head and the kid's arm just hangs in space and drops. The dad doesn't say a word.

Seeing that made me want to turn and run.

But I kept going to school and I saw this woman outside the doctor with a kid in a pram and she looked sick and she asks me for two bucks and I don't have two bucks to spare and she swears at me 'cause of what she thinks I have, that she doesn't. It's the morning the story has broken of those kids being killed in the playground and a couple are shopping at the IGA shake their heads as they point at the headline then they ignore the girl at the counter and make their way out. I see Sergeant on duty near the station telling a boy to pull up his socks and I can't see anything wrong with his socks but then I see Sergeant's holding a gun. There are teachers with guns up and down the street. Teachers with guns in class and snipers on the roof to protect the teachers who are protecting the kids. A woman out the front of the school with a sign that says: 'LEARNING STILL COUNTS'. The kids behind the fence are all targets for the terrorists and the organ thieves and the other kids who are not allowed in, the disaffected ones, and they are all so *angry* and so much better shots than the teachers because the teachers were marking when the disaffected were target practising. The public schools have run out of ammo and the kids from those schools are kept inside their homes or running feral with the radicalised. And then I'm hearing gunshots bang

bang

bang

bang

bang or is it fireworks for the centenary of the Greek club that got turned into a car wash? Shots one after the other

then something exploding in the sky.

Or is that just in my head 'cause nobody else is ducking down?

Do you ever feel like you don't know where to look?

JAMES: I …

MICHAEL: I didn't know where to look. Please hold me again. Don't let go of me now.

They hold one another as the light fades.

Then MICHAEL *is gone and* JAMES *is alone.*

TOBY *is on the other side.*

TOBY: I imagine Michael is in the bush. He has a lot of stuff going on

under the surface like a lot of people do. He is in the bush but he knows he is changing and he feels like / he needs to be near the sea.
MATT: / He needs to be in the sea. Nobody has noticed the changes happening to him. Nobody has asked: / What the hell is going on with you, Michael?
HENRY: / *What the hell is going on with you, Michael?*
TOBY: So he walks to the coast.
MATT: It takes him most of the day.
HENRY: As he walks he's planning how he'll just run across the sand and dive in. But when he gets to the beach, there are crowds of people everywhere.
TOBY: And he stops when he sees them all, he doesn't want this.
MATT: He hides in the bush at the top of a cliff.
HENRY: He watches all the people swimming and lying on the sand.
JAMES: All the people jogging and washing the beach off their toes at the tap by the road.
HENRY: He can hear this noise.
MATT: It's coming from underneath the water.
TOBY: Something calling him from under the sea.
JAMES: And he reaches down to feel his hands, and he sees that his skin has changed colour.
HENRY: It's gone from pink-grey to a kind of silver.
TOBY: And he goes to scratch his nose because there are flies eating a booger or something and his fingers don't feel his nose at all. His nose is gone.
MATT: He pulls his hands away from his face and looks down and sees his feet have changed colour and they seem small.
JAMES: He knows he really has to get to the water.
TOBY: He is not sure he can wait for everyone to leave the beach.
MATT: So he climbs up to the cliffs along from the beach and clambers around the side hoping nobody will look up and see him.
HENRY: But his feet are so small they can't support the weight of his legs and his hands have no grip now they feel like fins.
MATT: He gets stuck about a third of the way down the steep cliff. With little rocks falling down on the rocks below.
JAMES: He tries to hide, to keep still, but—
TOBY: A group of girls who sit on the rocks below look up.

KIERAN: The prettiest girl sees him there.
GIRL: *Oh my God, look at that.*
KIERAN: She says to her friends.
GIRL: *I know that loser. He went to my primary school.*
KIERAN: The girls stand up and point and they laugh and cheer and snap photographs of him.
GIRL: *Look at the sword sticking out of the front of his face.*
MATT: And when they see that his feet and his hands and his skin are weird they scream.
TOBY: People on the beach hear the screams and look up.
MATT: Everyone staring, pointing.
KIERAN: Michael needs to get into the sea.
JAMES: In the sea nobody will point at him and laugh.
HENRY: There will be no phones with cameras under the water.
KIERAN: No bitchy schools of fish.
TOBY: He wants a slide to appear so he can slide straight down into the sea but it doesn't.
KIERAN: Cathy the tallest girl in the group leaves the other girls.
TOBY: Cathy climbs up the cliff, she's sporty and makes it look easy, and so before she knows it she's next to Michael saying:
CATHY: *Are you alright? I'm not going to hurt you or say anything mean so please don't cut me with your sword. What's happened to you, to your skin?*
TOBY: It's complicated. Michael doesn't know what to say.
MATT: He tries to speak but all he can do is make a strange gurgling noise and one of his teeth drops out and clatters down the cliff face and lands near the girls and as they scream Cathy says:
CATHY: *You're turning into a swordfish.*
TOBY: I know, he says.
CATHY: *What's your name?*
JAMES: But he doesn't say his name.
HENRY: He stumbles and tumbles and splashes.
TOBY: As she sees him hit the blue and look up, she realises she's seen his face. She knows who the boy is.

    A long pause.

JAMES: I'm at Woolworths with Mum when I get a message.
TOBY: It's on TV on the morning news.

MATT: I get a text.
SAM: Mum wakes me up with this knock on the door, this look on her face.
GLEN / KIERAN: I find out on Facebook.
TRISTAN: I shut his page down.
KIERAN: Some idiot has liked the news about Michael.
JAMES: I knew. I knew because it had been too long since …

All the boys stand together and we hear the sea.

The holidays end.
GLEN: The weather's got cold now.
KIERAN: Sky grey.

Pause.

MATT: Monday morning first day back.
TOBY: Ibis stares as we walk down the road.
TRISTAN: Last term feels like years ago.
HENRY: Period one.
GLEN: Period two.
MATT: Then chairs in a line for a Year meeting.
KIERAN: Mr Harley smiles at us as we come in, take seats.
JAMES: Sit in lines.
SAM: Sergeant comes in.
TRISTAN: Aiden's on crutches now.
KIERAN: Simmo carries his bag.
MATT: Gavo's bleached his hair.
JAMES: Sampson scoffs a protein bar.
SAM: He's bulked up.
HENRY: Sargent says:
TRISTAN: *Welcome back, Year Twelve.*
KIERAN: He talks about the timetable change.
GLEN: Upcoming exam dates.
SAM: The musical tickets.
TRISTAN: Athletics carnival.
TOBY: Rowing.
MATT: Debating.
JAMES: Rugby.
KIERAN: Cross-country.

HENRY: Some new rules for boarders out of bounds.
JAMES: Why don't they just say it?
GLEN: What do they say?
SAM: What words can they say?
MATT: Why don't they just say his name?
JAMES: Footsteps.
GLEN: A kid stands in the door.
TOBY: A new kid.
KIERAN: Tall.
MATT: Black hair.
JAMES: Green eyes.
TRISTAN: Blond hair.
GLEN: Blue …
HENRY: New kid moves along the row.
JAMES: Takes a place.
MATT: Finds the space.
TOBY: Fills the empty chair.
JAMES: Sergeant looks at him a moment.
SAM: At the new kid.
JAMES: I don't know where to look.
MATT: Sergeant smiles at us and tells us his name.

Pause.

TOBY: And people stop mentioning Michael.
MATT: After saying his name so much it feels weird to bring him up.
HENRY: To talk about what he did.
SAM: What we didn't.
TOBY: The school says come and talk if we need …
HENRY: If we see an empty chair or his art work.
JAMES: If we are still thinking about him we should …
SAM / MATT: But we don't.
GLEN: I start to wonder if he existed in the first place.
JAMES: Like we only ever imagined him being there.
HENRY: Like they put his name on the roll one day as some kind of experiment of our memory, some sort of trick on our minds.
TOBY: And on the beach the waves roll in.
JAMES: It's cold today, nobody walks on the sand.

HENRY: The fish go about their business, swim between rocks and look up through the water / at the cloud.

TOBY: / At the cloud, stretching from the shore to the other side of the city, a question mark curls across the winter sky.

THE END

www.currency.com.au

Visit Currency Press' website now to:

- Buy your books online
- Browse through our full list of titles, from plays to screenplays, books on theatre, film and music, and more
- Choose a play for your school or amateur performance group by cast size and gender
- Obtain information about performance rights
- Find out about theatre productions and other performing arts news across Australia
- For students, read our study guides
- For teachers, access syllabus and other relevant information
- Sign up for our email newsletter

The performing arts publisher

www.ingramcontent.com/pod-product-compliance
Lightning Source LLC
Chambersburg PA
CBHW050023090426
42734CB00021B/3391